the every man series

being God's man...
as a satisfied single

Real Men. Real Life. Powerful Truth.

Stephen Arterburn, Kenny Luck, Todd Wendorff & Carl Moeller

WATERBROOK
PRESS

BEING GOD'S MAN…AS A SATISFIED SINGLE
PUBLISHED BY WATERBROOK PRESS
2375 Telstar Drive, Suite 160
Colorado Springs, Colorado 80920
A division of Random House, Inc.

ISBN 1-57856-683-5

Published in association with the literary agency of Alive Communications, Inc., 7680 Goddard Street, Suite 200, Colorado Springs, CO 80920.

Printed in the United States of America
2003—First Edition

10 9 8 7 6 5 4 3 2 1

contents

welcome to the every man
Bible study series

As Christian men, we crave true-to-life, honest, and revealing Bible study curricula that will equip us for the battles that rage in our lives. We are looking for resources that will get us into our Bibles in the context of mutually accountable relationships with other men. But like superheroes who wear masks and work hard to conceal their true identities, most of us find ourselves isolated and working alone on the major issues we face. Many of us present a carefully designed public self, while hiding our private self from view. This is not God's plan for us.

Let's face it. We all have trouble being honest with ourselves, particularly in front of other men.

As developers of a men's ministry, we believe that many of the problems among Christian men today are direct consequences of an inability to practice biblical openness—being honest about our struggles, questions, and temptations—and to connect with one another. Our external lives may be in order, but storms of unprocessed conflict, loss, and fear are eroding our resolve to maintain integrity. Sadly, hurting Christian men are flocking to unhealthy avenues of relief instead of turning to God's Word and to one another.

We believe the solution to this problem lies in creating opportunities for meaningful relationships among men. That's why we designed this Bible study series to be thoroughly interactive. When a man practices biblical openness with other men, he moves from secrecy to candor, from isolation to connection, and from pretense to authenticity.

Kenny and Todd developed the study sessions at Saddleback Church in Lake Forest, California, where they teach the men's morning Bible studies. There, men hear an outline of the Bible passage, read the verses together, and then answer a group discussion question at their small-group tables. The teaching pastor then facilitates further discussion within the larger group.

This approach is a huge success for many reasons, but the key is that, deep down, men really do want close friendships with other guys. We don't enjoy living on the barren islands of our own secret struggles. However, many men choose to process life, relationships, and pressures individually because they fear the vulnerability required in small-group gatherings. *Suppose someone sees behind my carefully constructed image? Suppose I encounter rejection after revealing one of my worst sins?* Men willingly take risks in business and the stock market, sports and recreation, but we do not easily risk our inner lives.

Many church ministries are now helping men win this battle, providing them with opportunities to experience Christian male companionship centered in God's Word. This study series aims to supplement and expand that good work around the country. If these lessons successfully reach you, then they will also reach every relationship and domain that you influence. That is our heartfelt prayer for every man in your group.

how to use this study guide

As you prepare for each session, first review the **Key Verse** and **Goals for Growth,** which reveal the focus of the study at hand. Discuss as a group whether or not you will commit to memorizing the Key Verse for each session. The **Head Start** section then explains why these goals are necessary and worthwhile. Each member of your small group should complete the **Connect with the Word** section *before* the small-group sessions. Consider this section to be your personal Bible study for the week. This will ensure that everyone has spent some time interacting with the biblical texts for that session and is prepared to share responses and personal applications. (You may want to mark or highlight any questions that were difficult or particularly meaningful, so you can focus on those during the group discussion.)

When you gather in your small group, you'll begin by reading aloud the **Head Start** section to remind everyone of the focus for the current session. The leader will then invite the group to share any questions, concerns, insights, or comments arising from their personal Bible study during the past week. If your group is large, consider breaking into subgroups of three or four people (no more than six) at this time.

Next get into **Connect with the Group,** starting with the **Group Opener.** These openers are designed to get at the heart of each week's lesson. They focus on how the men in your group relate to the passage and topic you are about to discuss. The group leader will read the opener for that week's session aloud and then facilitate interaction on the **Discussion Questions** that follow. (Remember: Not everyone has to offer an answer for every question.)

Leave time after your discussion to complete the **Standing Strong** exercises, which challenge each man to consider, *What's my next move?* As you openly express your thoughts to the group, you'll be able to hold one another accountable to reach for your goals.

Finally, close in **prayer**, either in your subgroups or in the larger group. You may want to use this time to reflect on and respond to what God has done in your group during the session. Also invite group members to share their personal joys and concerns, and use this as "grist" for your prayer time together.

By way of review, each lesson is divided into the following sections:

To be read or completed *before* the small-group session:
- **Key Verse**
- **Goals for Growth**
- **Head Start**
- **Connect with the Word** (home Bible study: 30-40 minutes)

To be completed *during* the small-group session:
- Read aloud the **Head Start** section (5 minutes)
- Discuss personal reaction to **Connect with the Word** (10 minutes)
- **Connect with the Group** (includes the **Group Opener** and discussion of the heart of the lesson: 30-40 minutes)
- **Standing Strong** (includes having one person pray for the group; challenges each man to take action: 20 minutes)

what is a satisfied single man?

You may be single by choice or as a result of circumstances. You may have future plans to marry and have a family, or you may sense that God is calling you to a life of singleness. No matter what your situation is, God's will for you right now is to be content as a single and to trust that this is His plan for you at this time in your life. How will you respond to your singleness? What will you learn from it? And how will you survive the temptations confronting every single person in our world today?

You know firsthand that single men face unique spiritual and moral struggles in today's culture. That's why developing a strong and godly character is so critical. In fact, it's the cornerstone of being God's man. To be successful in living out your commitment to Christ as a single man, you must master the issues of sexual integrity, isolation, contentment, spiritual warfare, and your identity in Christ. *Being God's Man...as a Satisfied Single* is designed to help you do just that.

This study focuses on the lives of eight men in Scripture who were single for a lifetime or at least for a significant part of their lives.

How did these men approach the issues of life that all single men face? Some of these biblical characters, such as Daniel, Nehemiah, and Paul, are positive examples. Jonah, on the other hand, struggled with character issues. Some men such as Timothy are well known, while others—such as Zerubbabel, Boaz, and Jonathan—are less well known. Each man faced the pressures and character challenges that are unique to single men.

Our goal in this study is to stimulate personal reflection and honest dialogue with God and with other men about these matters. As you work through each session, you'll do more than just absorb information; you'll be challenged to think through the biblical principles that address the issues single men face as well as their practical applications to your life. We encourage you to do this study in a small group where you'll find support and encouragement to put these principles into daily practice as you interact with other guys who are dealing with the same issues. But whether you choose to do this study individually or in a group, realize that complete honesty with yourself, with God, and with others will produce the greatest results.

Our prayer is that you will embrace God's plan for you as a single man and that you will experience His joy in your journey toward becoming a satisfied single.

real love
on the threshing-room floor

Boaz

Key Verse

I have told the men not to touch you. (Ruth 2:9)

Goals for Growth

- Understand the basis for maintaining sexual integrity.
- Recognize the role of restraint in our sexuality.
- Develop habits that honor the women in our lives.

Head Start

Imagine this scenario: You are a financially successful single man, your business interests are prospering, and you have great influence in your community. At the height of another successful business season, you are alone in the office late at night, taking a well-deserved snooze. Something wakes you up. It's a beautiful woman, dressed to the nines, lying at your feet...

Surely this is a dream, you think. But it's for real. And no one else is around. What would you do? Boaz found himself in exactly this position, and yet he found the strength to maintain his sexual integrity.

For most single men, the temptation to compromise sexually is a powerful and ever-present reality. We often find ourselves in situations where it's easy to compromise, to let the bar slide down a bit. We can rationalize and make excuses, or we can keep our eyes on the reward of obeying God by maintaining our sexual integrity.

This is a cutting-edge issue for today's single man. Let's see how a man of God handled it.

Connect with the Word

Read Ruth 2:1,4-8,14-16.

1. Describe Boaz from the details provided in these verses.

2. What can you say about Boaz's character?

3. What was Boaz concerned about?

Read Ruth 3.

4. In this chapter Boaz found himself in a situation that could have resulted in sexual compromise with Ruth. What character qualities did Boaz demonstrate in the way he treated Ruth?

5. What would you have done in a similar situation?

6. What do you think Boaz did to exercise restraint in his relationship with Ruth?

7. Ruth's mother-in-law sent Ruth to Boaz and told her what she should do. Why do you think Naomi felt confident that Boaz would not dishonor Ruth?

8. Do you think your reputation with women is as honorable as Boaz's? Why or why not?

Connect with the Group

Group Opener

Read the group opener aloud and discuss the questions that follow. (Suggestion: As you begin your group discussion time in each of the following sessions, consider forming smaller groups of three to six men. This will allow more time for discussion and give everyone an opportunity to share their thoughts and struggles.)

Late night fun—a nice dinner together and a hilarious movie. Tom found that he and Heather tracked together on so many things. She was easy to talk and laugh with, and she loved to mountain bike even more than he did—if that were possible. And their time together had proven that they shared the same warped sense of humor. When they arrived back at her apartment, Heather asked him to come up. What's the problem with that? Just a little harmless TV on the couch, right?

But the focus on the couch quickly moved from *Late Night* to each other, and Tom found himself rapidly rationalizing his desire to stay the night. *It's all right*, he thought. *She doesn't have to work tomorrow, and neither do I… No one keeps tabs on us… She could be the type of girl I'd like to marry someday anyway.*

Yet something didn't seem quite right about the whole thing— sort of like the stereo salesman who presses his point too strongly about why "You just have to buy this stereo today." Tom knew he was no longer "getting to know" Heather, but was instead responding to his biological impulses. If God was central in his life most of the time, He sure wasn't right now.

Tom stood up. He took a deep breath and said, "Hey, tonight was great, Heather. I am so glad we connected! God must have known we would click. I really don't want anything to derail this, so I'm going to head home now. But let's talk tomorrow…um…later today, okay?"

Discussion Questions

a. Analyze Tom's thinking, behavior, and responses. With what do you agree or disagree? What might you have done in a similar situation?

b. Where do your sexual temptations most often come from? Which temptations do you find most challenging these days? What is most helpful to you in resisting them?

c. Share your thoughts on what it means to "honor one another" in your relationships with women. (See Romans 12:10.)

d. What key principles do you find in Boaz's example that can help you keep your sexual integrity intact? (Try to list at least four.)

Standing Strong

What specific steps will you take this week to strengthen your commitment to sexual integrity?

Write a prayer expressing your desire to live a godly life, particularly in the area of sexuality.

Ask someone in your group to hold you accountable in this area this week.

character and confidence under fire

Daniel

Key Verse

They could find no corruption in him, because he was trustworthy and neither corrupt nor negligent. Finally these men said, "We will never find any basis for charges against this man Daniel unless it has something to do with the law of his God." (Daniel 6:4-5)

Goals for Growth

- Recognize the source of real strength: integrity.
- Realize that both God and men honor those with integrity.
- Develop the true confidence and boldness that come from godly character.

Head Start

Daniel in the lion's den. That old Sunday-school Bible story always comes to mind whenever we talk about Daniel. We know God rescued him from the lions, but how did he get into that situation in the first place? In the final analysis, it was his character that got him into trouble. The only charge envious politicians could level at Daniel was that he was devoted to his God. In other words, his character was unassailable. Try judging most of today's leaders by that standard, and they'll fall far short.

As men we are often faced with situations that tempt us to cheat, to shave a bit off the edges when we think no one will notice. But when we develop a habit of inconsistency and dishonesty, we also experience the subtle fears of being discovered. We become confused and lose our self-confidence. We don't risk because we'd risk exposure.

But godly character breeds confidence. When we live with integrity—when our walk matches our talk—we live boldly, speak boldly, and act boldly. That's a real man—like Daniel.

Connect with the Word

Read Daniel 1:8; 2:14-23; 5:10-17; 6:1-5.

1. According to these passages, which of Daniel's character qualities remained consistent throughout his life?

2. Daniel was politically successful and powerful, and he proved to
   be a durable leader, outlasting the reigns of at least three rulers in
   two separate dynasties. How do you think Daniel was able to
   maintain highly influential political positions throughout his
   long life, even when rulers and empires changed?

3. Daniel said to King Belshazzar, "You may keep your gifts for
   yourself and give your rewards to someone else" (5:17). What
   enabled Daniel to speak so boldly to a king?

4. Which of Daniel's character qualities do you most admire?

5. What do you like best about your own character? What do you
   think God likes most about you?

6. What areas of your character need improvement? What can you do to develop these areas with the help of the Holy Spirit?

Connect with the Group

Group Opener

Consider your work environment for a moment, then rewrite Daniel 6:4-5 to reflect your coworkers' view of you. Share what you wrote with the group.

Discussion Questions

a. Consider Daniel's boldness as described in Daniel 1:8. (Our best guess is that Daniel was about thirteen years old when this took place.) Daniel and his friends were to be fed with the king's rich food and wine as part of their leadership training. There was just one problem. God's Law forbade them to eat the food—it wasn't kosher. In responding to this situation, where did Daniel place his confidence?

b. Reread Daniel 5:17. Why do you think Daniel rejected the king's rewards? What did this reflect about his character?

c. Daniel's boldness never seemed to falter. What was his response when he was asked to compromise his spiritual habits (6:10)? How would you have handled the situation?

d. What kinds of situations challenge a single guy's confidence or courage these days? What kinds of challenges have you faced? Be specific.

e. What advice or encouragement can you offer to one another in dealing with these challenges? What would you like to pray for one another?

Standing Strong

In what ways have you compromised your convictions this past week? In what situations have you been bold?

Based on what you learned from this week's study, what aspect(s) of your character do you want to strengthen this week? What steps will you take?

Is there a specific area in your life in which you would like to become bolder? Write it down below, then share this desire with another man in the group. Pray for one another, asking Christ to develop His character in your lives so that you will live boldly like Daniel.

dynamic balance

Nehemiah

Key Verse

Then I said to them, "You see the trouble we are in: Jerusalem lies in ruins, and its gates have been burned with fire. Come, let us rebuild the wall of Jerusalem, and we will no longer be in disgrace." I also told them about the gracious hand of my God upon me and what the king had said to me.

They replied, "Let us start rebuilding." So they began this good work. (Nehemiah 2:17-18)

Goals for Growth

- Realize that balance is the key to a healthy view of work.
- Understand that work is good, but God produces the results.
- Commit to unleashing the power of godly balance in our work.

Head Start

Many times I (Carl) have heard people say things like, "A truly successful life is a balanced life." In our busy lives as single men, the idea of living a balanced life is especially hard to grasp. We think of playground seesaws taking us on a jarring ride all the way from the top right down to the bottom. Or we envision a delicate scientific scale where one microgram swings the meter way out of whack. Our lives are much too chaotic to make sense of these pictures of "balance."

But perhaps we can find a better word picture to use.

Awhile back I went to get the tires on my car rotated. As I watched, the mechanic removed one of my tires and placed it on a machine that spun it at highway speeds. Then he took the tire off the machine and placed some small weights around the rim. When I asked what he was doing, he called it "dynamic balancing," an adjustment that keeps the tires from vibrating everything else in the car, which would eventually cause damage.

Isn't that a better description of our lives as single men? We're often spinning around furiously, gathering more and more responsibility. If things get out of kilter just a bit, a damaging wobble develops. If things get off balance even more, major damage results.

For single men, one of the most common "unbalancers" is our work life. We think, *Why not stay the extra hours?* But we must strive to see that even a strong work ethic, while good, becomes dangerous when it causes an imbalance in other areas of our lives.

I think that's what Nehemiah faced: an important, yet all-consuming project that threatened to throw his life completely out of whack. But by maintaining dynamic balance and wisely distributing the work load, Nehemiah was able to maneuver safely over some pretty rough roads—just like my tires.

Connect with the Word

Read Nehemiah 3:1-27.

1. The work of rebuilding the walls of Jerusalem was delegated and divided among many families. In what ways did Nehemiah demonstrate a balanced approach as he tackled this huge project?

2. Describe a time, if any, when you faced a similarly daunting challenge. How balanced was your approach? What could you have done a little better? What lessons did you learn from the experience?

Read Nehemiah 5:17-19.

3. Nehemiah was a recognized leader and a great inspiration to his people during this project. How did he show his devotion to them in this passage?

Read Nehemiah 6:15-16.

4. According to verse 16, who got the real credit for Nehemiah's success? What effect did this realization have on Israel's enemies?

5. Describe a time when God helped you succeed in some area of your life. Take a moment right now to give God credit for your accomplishments and offer Him your thanks.

Connect with the Group

Group Opener

Calculate the amount of time you devoted to each of the following areas last week. Remember that you have only 168 total hours!

Work:

Leisure Activities:

Spiritual Growth/Ministry:

Rest:

Relationships:

Discussion Questions

a. In what ways does your life seem to be out of balance lately?

b. If you could, in what areas of your life would you cut back the amount of time you spend? Where would you like to invest more time? Why?

c. What steps will you take this week to get your life back in balance? How will you redistribute your time?

Standing Strong

Share with the group the results of your personal time calculation from the group opener. Discuss what your calculation reveals about the priorities in your life. (If you think it might help, draw a pie chart and indicate what percentage you think each of these areas—work, ministry, relationships, rest—represents in your life.) Ask group members to share their observations about your strengths and weaknesses. Ask them how they think you might better divide your time and where they think you have a tendency to get out of balance.

Pray for one another and ask God to help each of you become more dynamically balanced. Ask someone in your group to hold you accountable this week as you take steps to reprioritize your activities and redistribute your time. Set up a time to talk about your progress.

the courage to care

Jonathan

Key Verse

Jonathan made a covenant with David because he loved him as himself. (1 Samuel 18:3)

Goals for Growth

- Understand the purpose and benefits of accountability with other men.
- Develop habits that will encourage greater accountability.
- Discover new ways to become significantly connected to other men.

Head Start

Our society paints a weird picture of what a "real man" is. Imagine a guy, his face set against the biting wind, alone and conquering all—

the picture of a rugged individualist who doesn't need anything or anyone. The truth is, being a loner in this world can get pretty lonesome! As men, we often have a tough time connecting authentically with one another, and a major reason is this false image of what a real man should be.

The book of Ecclesiastes says, "If one falls down, his friend can help him up. But pity the man who falls and has no one to help him up!" (4:10). Don't skip over the profound implications of this verse: Men who recognize their need for true friends will have someone to pick them up when they fall. When loners fall, they're totally on their own.

So avoid getting caught in the "real men don't..." trap. You know what we're talking about. "Real men don't show their emotions" or "Real men don't care about the needs of others. They just get what they want." But the truth is, *real* "real men" *do* connect with other men because they see the awesome benefits of such fellowship. Real men know that to succeed they need others.

Jonathan, David's best friend, knew that too. He understood that even though he was the king's son and heir to the throne of Israel, he really needed a close friend. Jonathan probably saw in David the godly leadership qualities that were so lacking in his father, Saul. And in recognizing that God's blessing had left the house of Saul, Jonathan was, in fact, acknowledging his allegiance to David.

Look closely at Jonathan. You'll see a real man caring enough to connect.

Connect with the Word

Read 1 Samuel 18:1-4; 19:1-7; 20.

1. What qualities do you think Jonathan saw in David that were so appealing?

2. Given all the benefits Jonathan enjoyed as a prince of Israel, what pressures do you think he faced?

3. Based upon this passage, what character qualities do you think Jonathan possessed?

4. Standing up to his father, the king, on David's behalf was risky and took a great deal of courage (19:4-5). Why do you think Jonathan risked so much to save David?

Connect with the Group

Group Opener
Read the group opener aloud and discuss the questions that follow.

I [Kenny] remember traveling to Alabama after my freshman year of college to visit my brother Lance. A year earlier, Lance had helped me understand what it meant to know Christ personally, so I was looking forward to bringing him up to date on how my life had changed since that fateful day. In a word, I wanted to reconnect with my brother and catch up.

After a long plane trip to Alabama, I arrived to see an excited brother wrap me in a bear hug. Once at Lance's place, we burned the midnight oil by playing records and eating and talking about everything from God to guitars. The evening was absolutely magical until...Lance whipped out a cigarette.

"What's that?" I asked.

"A cigarette. What do you think it is?"

"Why are you smoking?"

"I only smoke about a pack a week."

"But you shouldn't be smoking." I pulled out the Bible Lance had bought for me a year earlier. "Doesn't it say here that your body is a temple to be used by God? It's right here in Corinthians."

Then Lance did something I didn't expect him to do. He took the unlit cigarette, snapped it in two, threw it in the trash, and said, "Well, that's that, then."

Unbelievable....

Without hesitation, without any debate, and without any nicotine patch (NicoDerm hadn't been invented yet), my brother quit smoking cold turkey and hasn't put another cancer stick in his mouth in more than twenty years. Looking back through time, I am bowled over by the fact that Lance stuck with his commitment to stop smoking. The impetus was what a fellow brother in Christ said to him. Believe me, after seeing what Lance did that night, I felt *connected* to him.[1]

Discussion Questions

a. What, if anything, in this case study can you identify with? Which of the two characters do you relate to most? Why?

b. What principles or insights stand out as the most relevant and/or personally applicable from the Scripture passage in this study?

---

1. Stephen Arterburn and Kenny Luck, *Every Man, God's Man* (Colorado Springs: WaterBrook Press, 2003), 143-4.

c. Describe the closest friendship you have right now. What qualities do you value most in your friend? If you don't have a close friend, what can you do to nurture one of your casual friendships?

d. What is the extent of your connection with other men? Who knows what your daily struggles are?

e. In what ways have you sought to build friendships for the right reasons, not just for appearances? Are you still pretending that you can handle everything on your own? Explain. What steps can you take to overcome this tendency and begin making real connections with other men?

Standing Strong
List the steps you will take to build deeper friendships with other men this week.

Write the name of one man with whom you'd like to begin building a quality friendship in the year ahead.

fishy, slimy, and all washed-up

Jonah

Key Verse

Jonah ran away from the LORD and headed for Tarshish. He went down to Joppa, where he found a ship bound for that port. After paying the fare, he went aboard and sailed for Tarshish to flee from the LORD. (Jonah 1:3)

Goals for Growth

- Learn to recognize and resist self-centeredness and selfishness.
- Understand how genuine dependability and responsibility develop.
- Realize how God views our selfish behavior.

Head Start

"But you said you'd be there. I waited an hour!"
"You promised you'd call! Now look what happened!"

"Why didn't you show up? I really needed you!"

Ever hear words like that? They can be devastating, especially to a valued relationship. Yet the reality for most of us is that we do let people down. We forget; we mess up. But keeping our word is the primary requisite for dependability, and dependability requires that we put others first.

The business world uses a little acronym WIIFM that's loaded with meaning: What's in It for ME? This is the basic question many businesses train their sales force to answer for their potential clients. It plays into a fundamental truth about human beings: *We are self-centered!* We want everything to revolve around *us*, to meet *our* expectations, to fulfill *our* dreams. For a salesperson, finding the WIIFM for each customer can be the key to closing a sale.

It's been said that most single women are looking for someone or something they can depend on, and most single men want to *play*. We're out to have fun! And while play is okay for a while, too much play tends to make us less diligent and dependable. We tend to get more and more self-centered and self-absorbed as we look for the next fun activity. That can be our biggest obstacle to living full on and full out for God.

But in God's world, *you* are not the center of the universe. Jonah had to learn that lesson the hard way—in the belly of a great fish. The bottom line is: To be God's man, you must see the benefit of being someone others can depend on.

Connect with the Word

Read Jonah 1.

1. What do Jonah's actions reveal about his basic view of life? Describe his attitude.

2. Jonah said he worshiped the God of heaven (verse 9), but in what ways did his actions contradict this claim and reveal a hard, selfish heart?

3. What finally motivated Jonah to respond to God's call?

4. When have you had an attitude like Jonah's? What were the consequences?

Read Jonah 4:1-11.

5. How did God respond to Jonah's selfishness? What changes needed to take place in Jonah's heart to make him a dependable man?

6. How is your relationship with God affected when you choose a purely self-centered route to get what you want?

7. What changes in your view of God need to take place to help you loosen your grip on self-interest?

8. Why didn't Jonah believe that God had his best interests in mind?

9. Are you convinced that God loves you unconditionally? Why or why not? In what ways do you currently experience His love and presence in your life? (*Suggestion:* Explore these questions over the course of several weeks, and spend some time focusing on God's loving presence.)

Connect with the Group

Group Opener
Read the group opener aloud and discuss the questions that follow.

It wasn't just the fact that we'd been advertising the event for weeks or that we had committed resources and expected a huge turnout, but the most disappointing thing was that we had confirmed the event just a few days before...

Our campus ministry had invited a nationally known star athlete, who had just won the Heisman Trophy, to give his testimony as a Christian to hundreds of our student athletes. Since he was going to be in town for a special dinner, we connected with him and told him about our plans weeks ahead of time. He agreed to come, and we confirmed the event two days before he arrived.

On the day of the event, we went to his hotel at the scheduled time to pick him up, but he wasn't there. His agent said he was "otherwise engaged." When I (Carl) asked where he was, I found out that he was at a local restaurant.

Two hours before the event was scheduled to begin, I caught up with the football player and confronted him.

"Hi! Remember me?" I said. "We're really looking forward to having you speak for us. We have a couple hundred athletes coming out to hear you."

"Uh, well…I just don't think I can make it. I'm kinda committed, ya know, to…"

"But this will really let us down. Won't you make it for just twenty minutes or so?"

"Sorry, man. Can't do it."

Eventually I had to scramble for an alternative program and go in front of the crowd to apologize for the change in plans. God worked in spite of the athlete's irresponsibility, but I find it interesting that I never heard of his Christian testimony again.

Discussion Questions

a. Describe a time, if ever, when someone let you down this way. When have you let another person down?

b. What contributes to your own selfish behavior? What can you do to avoid focusing entirely on your own needs and interests?

c. What effect does the irresponsibility of others have on you? How have you responded in the past when someone else's irresponsibility affected you?

d. How would you define *selfless dependability?* What would it look like to you?

e. Would you hire Jonah? Why or why not? How would you challenge him to become more trustworthy and dependable?

f. In what ways does our view of God affect how we respond to Him? For many of us, what seems to be lacking in our view of God?

Standing Strong

Discuss with the group the importance of being someone others can depend on. What key points did you pick up from this week's lesson that you can apply to your life? What steps will you take this week to become more dependable?

Pray for one another this week, asking God to show each of you where you are self-centered and to help you become the kind of dependable and other-focused person He wants you to be.

content in any situation

Paul

Key Verse

I know what it is to be in need, and I know what it is to have plenty.
I have learned the secret of being content in any…situation, whether
well fed or hungry, whether living in plenty or in want. I can do everything through him who gives me strength. (Philippians 4:12-13)

Goals for Growth

- Learn how to be content in any situation.
- Understand how to access God's peace.
- Recognize what causes us to lose our perspective and peace.

Head Start

The most common aspects of life today are unsettledness, chaos, and
change. In fact, the one constant in life seems to be change. On top

of that, you can often find yourself experiencing what Larry Crabb has called "shattered dreams." The things you hoped and prayed for just haven't worked out. The job you wanted didn't come through. The woman you wanted to spend every waking moment with didn't want to see you again. The money you needed just wasn't there.

A few years back, I (Carl) was doing great in my job. I was bringing in 25 percent more than my goal, and the organization was experiencing unprecedented growth. But even so, some unethical practices had begun to surface in company leadership.

One Friday afternoon, out of the blue, the vice president handed me a memo of totally false statements that were being used as a pretext for dismissing me. She gave me no options and asked for my resignation. I was completely blindsided and felt as if I'd been kicked in the gut. If I had truly failed, I would have understood, but this was fundamentally unfair and downright wrong.

Crushed and confused, I prayed and laid the entire situation before God over the following days and weeks. As I sought Him in my pain and emptiness, He began to show me that if I had continued working in that environment, I would eventually have compromised my convictions. He had allowed this situation, unfair as it was, to move me closer to the center of His will for my life. This realization helped me surrender the situation entirely to Him, and gradually His peace began to fill my life.

In a few months, God provided me with a better and more fulfilling position elsewhere. His patience and wisdom enabled me to live faithfully and consistently during a tough time—and even offer comfort to others in similar job-loss situations.

There are many situations in life that can cause us to lose our peace and spiritual perspective. We may even be tempted to believe that God has abandoned us or that our lives are meaningless. And yet when life is going great and we're enjoying tremendous opportunities, we may still feel a nagging emptiness that robs us of peace with God. The challenge is to find our way to the eye of the storm and ask: *How can I have peace of mind regardless of what's going on around me?* The apostle Paul found that path to peace. His experience can help us navigate through life, no matter what the weather.

Connect with the Word

Read 2 Corinthians 1:3-9.

1. Think about some of Paul's worst crises or pressures. Where was God's comfort during those times?

2. How did Paul find strength to endure his trials?

3. In what ways did Paul offer help or comfort to those going through similar trials?

4. In what areas of your life do you feel "uncomforted" as a result of your trials? What encouragement do you find from Paul's example?

5. How will you seek God's comfort in these areas?

6. According to verse 9, Paul was learning to rely on God rather than himself. What, in practical terms, would reliance on God look like in your life?

Read 2 Corinthians 11:22-29.

7. Beatings, stonings, being cast out of cities, rejection—how would you feel under those circumstances?

8. What are your current sufferings like compared to Paul's? Share any insights you've gained from this comparison.

9. Think about mental or emotional suffering. Do you think this kind of suffering is worse than Paul's physical sufferings? Why or why not?

10. Is it possible to have peace and contentment in any circumstance? Explain. When have you experienced this peace that passes understanding? (See Philippians 4:7.)

11. What do these verses reveal about God's desire to provide for you in any situation?

Connect with the Group

Group Opener

How would you define *contentment?* Think back on your life. When have you felt the most content? What factors do you think contributed to your contentment? When have you felt least content? Why do you think this was the case?

Discussion Questions

a. The word *happiness* comes from the same root as "to happen" or "circumstance." In what ways does biblical joy differ from happiness?

b. Paul was a single man his entire adult life. What do you think was the key to Paul's contentment as a single adult? What evidence of contentment did he give? (*Hint:* See 1 Corinthians 7:7-8.) In what ways are you like Paul in this area? How are you different?

c. In what other areas of your life do you struggle most with contentment?

d. What can you do to experience the kind of godly contentment and joy Paul experienced?

Standing Strong

What is your level of contentment these days? Are you restless or resting? Explain.

Connect with another man in the group this week and discuss your level of contentment in the areas of your life where you struggle most. Pray for each other and hold each other accountable for the steps you've committed to take to become more content. (Review your answers in the group opener.)

power in purpose

Zerubbabel

Key Verse

Zerubbabel, Jeshua and the rest of the heads of the families of Israel answered, "You have no part with us in building a temple to our God. We alone will build it for the LORD, the God of Israel, as King Cyrus, the king of Persia, commanded us." (Ezra 4:3)

Goals for Growth

- Realize that God has designed each of us for a unique purpose.
- Recognize that when we focus on our true purpose in life, we tap in to God's power to accomplish what He wants us to do.
- Identify ways to zero in on the important things in our lives.

Head Start

I (Carl) recently bought a laser pointer to help me with presentations. It reminded me of how incredible light is. With this little pointer I can send a concentrated beam of red light all the way across a large room to where I need it! And all that power is generated by a little AAA battery! A regular flashlight using the same battery produces only a weak, diffused light. The light from a pointer is more powerful because it is focused.

When you were a kid, did you ever try to burn a hole in a leaf with a magnifying glass and some sunlight? I used to do that, and I was always amazed that I could set the leaf smoldering with just a little sunlight, even on a cold day. (Good thing I never set anything on fire!) That power from the sun was there all along; it just needed to be focused in order for anything to happen.

This week's session is about a man, not well known to many, who had a similar type of intense focus. Zerubbabel was commissioned and committed to bring the Israelites back to Jerusalem from captivity in Babylon to rebuild the temple. With his complete dedication to that purpose and his single-minded focus on serving God, he refused to let anything else get in his way.

As single men we can easily lose our focus and find our strength depleted. But we must remember that our power comes from being focused—like my laser pointer or a magnifying glass. When we focus on God's purpose for our lives and seek His power to accomplish the things He's called us to do, then we can really set things on fire.

Connect with the Word

Read Ezra 4:1-5.

1. Zerubbabel's reply to those who would have liked to help in the rebuilding of the temple was pretty blunt. Why do you think he rebuked them?

2. What does verse 3 reveal about Zerubbabel's focus?

3. In what ways did Zerubbabel's passion correspond with God's passion for the purity of His temple?

Read Haggai 2:1-9.

4. According to this passage, what do you think Zerubbabel received from the Lord that enabled him to lead the people and rebuild the temple?

5. Why would hearing God's words spoken through the prophet Haggai give Zerubbabel increased power and focus?

Read Zechariah 4:1-10.

6. When Zerubbabel finished rebuilding the temple, the people rejoiced. Who ultimately received the credit for rebuilding the temple (verse 9)?

7. Reread verse 6. What do you think the point of this verse is? How does it relate to our plans and purposes?

Connect with the Group

Group Opener

Ask each group member to describe what *focus* and *purpose* in life mean to him. Be practical!

Discussion Questions

a. What similarities are there, if any, between your descriptions and the life of Zerubbabel?

b. In what ways does God honor our complete dependence on Him?

c. For a moment, imagine being God. Describe in a sentence or two what you think He views as most important in your life right now? How do you think He sees you?

d. What keeps you from surrendering to and serving God? Be specific.

e. Which of these barriers will you work to scratch off your list this week? What steps will you take to do this?

Standing Strong

What is your primary passion for serving God? What is one way you want to see Him use you in the future? Share your answers with one other man in the group.

Give that man permission to call you sometime this week to ask how you're doing with making your desire come to fruition.

true identity revealed

Timothy

Key verse

You then, my son, be strong in the grace that is in Christ Jesus. (2 Timothy 2:1)

Goals for Growth

- Understand that with Christ living in us, we have all that we need for life.
- Recognize attitudes and habits that keep us from living in the power we already have.
- See the potential we have when we live in the power of Christ.

Head Start

"It's easy; just step back."

Standing with my back to the cliff, sweat dripping off my head, I (Carl) was getting ready to rappel down. The advice didn't help. *Much easier said than done!* I thought.

But my rock-climbing instructor reminded me of all the rope, webbing, and hardware that held me tight. I took a deep breath, looked up, leaned back, and hopped out into the gaping space below me. And I swung out and down—WOW! The rope played out, and I was *walking* down the cliff. Spider-Man had nothing on me!

It wasn't long before I was bouncing side to side, even running a few steps along the cliff in an arc. An incredible sense of exhilaration and freedom filled me as I played myself down the rock face. Once at the bottom, I just couldn't wait to get back on top and do it again. And each time, the climb up became easier because I knew what fun it was to rappel back down.

I was in an unnatural situation, but I had all the resources I needed to accomplish the task. And once I released myself to it, I was filled with incredible power and joy.

The biblical Timothy's experience was a lot like that. He was young and fearful and found himself in a situation that was way beyond his experience. He needed someone to remind him of all the resources available to him. He needed to be convinced of who he truly was in Christ. This study will take you into the heart of someone who needed to face his fears and live in Christ's power.

Connect with the Word

Read 2 Timothy 2:1-7.

1. What was Paul doing for Timothy in this passage?

2. Focus on verse 1 for a moment. What can we do on a daily basis to be "strong in…grace"? Be specific.

3. How should you "endure hardship" in the days ahead (verse 3)? What will help you remember that God is present with you to provide strength and comfort?

4. Paul used some word pictures to remind Timothy of who he truly was in Christ. What character qualities was he trying to highlight in each of the following descriptions:

soldier (verses 3 and 4)

athlete (verse 5)

farmer (verse 6)

5. As you reflect on these qualities, how do you think Christ's grace (verse 1) can help you as you seek to live in His power?

Connect with the Group

Group Opener
Read the group opener aloud and discuss the questions that follow.

Does Hoover Dam generate power! Check out these impressive statistics:

- Water falls 530 feet into the seventeen enormous Francis-type vertical hydraulic turbines, which have a rated capacity of three million horsepower.
- Seventeen generators with a capacity of 388,000 kilowatts convert the rotations of the water turbines from mechanical power to electricity.
- In the record-setting year of 1984, the Hoover power plant yielded a net generation of 10,348,020,000 (that's billion with a *b*) kilowatt-hours of power.
- Eleven cities in Nevada, Arizona, and Southern California rely on Hoover-generated kilowatts to light and power their communities, benefiting millions of people.

The numbers are so huge that we cannot fathom how much power those generators produce. Yet all of that incredible power is barely a drop in the bucket compared to the vast reservoir of power readily available to God's man: the power of prayer. Check this out:

Now to him who is able to do immeasurably *more* than all we ask or imagine, according to his power that is at work within *us*. (Ephesians 3:20, [emphasis added])

Inside of every God's man there is a living, breathing vortex of supernatural power.[2]

Discussion Questions

a. Talk about the manifestations of God's power you've seen in creation. (For example, have you ever been to Niagara Falls or some other awesome creation or natural wonder?)

b. What does it mean to you to have God's power residing in you? When are you most aware of His abiding presence? When do you tend to forget about it? Why?

---

2. Arterburn and Luck, *Every Man, God's Man,* 173-4.

c. Name one person who has built you up, encouraged your walk with Christ, or reminded you of your God-given potential. How specifically has this person encouraged you?

d. Name one man you are encouraging these days. In what specific ways are you encouraging him? Who would you like to share a word of encouragement with? Why did you choose this person? In what specific ways would you like to build him up?

e. What are your strengths? What are some of the weaknesses you
   see in yourself? List some of your weak areas and then write out
   the strengths you find in Christ that counter those weaknesses.

My Weaknesses	*Christ's Strength*

Standing Strong
Dream big! In what area of your life do you think God wants to move next to develop your identity in Christ? Share this with one other man in your group. If you're not sure, ask God to show you what He wants to do next. Pray for each other this week as you seek to develop your real identity in Christ.

This week, call the person you shared with and let him know how he has encouraged you.

small-group resources

leader tips

What if men aren't doing the Connect with the Word section before our small-group session?

Don't be discouraged. You set the pace. If you are doing the study and regularly referring to it in conversations with your men through-out the week, they will pick up on its importance. Here are some suggestions to motivate the men in your group to do their home Bible study:

- Send out a midweek e-mail in which you share your answer to one of the study questions. This shows them that you are personally committed to and involved in the study.

- Ask the guys to hit "respond to all" on their e-mail program and share one insight from that week's Bible study with the entire group. Encourage them to send it out before the next small-group session.

- Every time you meet, ask each man in the group to share one insight from his home study.

What if men are not showing up for small group?

This might mean they are losing a sin battle and don't want to admit it to the group. Or they might be consumed with other priorities. Or maybe they don't think they're getting anything out of the group. Here are some suggestions for getting the guys back each week:

- Affirm them when they show up, and tell them how much it means to you that they make small group a priority.

- From time to time, ask them to share one reason they think small group is important to them.
- Regularly call or send out an e-mail the day before you meet to remind them you're looking forward to seeing them.
- Check in with any guy who has missed more than one session, and find out what's going on in his life.
- Get some feedback from the men. You may need to adjust your style. Listen and learn.

What if group discussion is not happening?

You are a discussion facilitator. You have to keep guys involved in the discussion or you'll lose them. You can engage a man who isn't sharing by saying, "Chuck, you've been quiet. What do you think about this question or discussion?" You should also be prepared to share your own personal stories that are related to the discussion questions. You'll set the example by the kind of sharing you do.

What if one man is dominating the group time?

You have to deal with it. If you don't, men will stop showing up. No one wants to hear from just one guy all the time. It will quickly kill morale. Meet with the guy in person and privately. Firmly but gently suggest that he allow others more time to talk. Be positive and encouraging, but truthful. You might say, "Bob, I notice how enthusiastic you are about the group and how you're always prepared to share your thoughts with the group. But there are some pretty quiet guys in the group too. Have you noticed? Would you be willing to help me get them involved in speaking up?"

How do I get the guys in my group more involved?

Give them something to do. Ask one guy to bring a snack. Invite another to lead the prayer time (ask in advance). Have one guy sub for you one week as the leader. (Meet with him beforehand to walk through the group program and the time allotments for each segment.) Encourage another guy to lead a subgroup.

What if guys are not being vulnerable during the Standing Strong or prayer times?

You model openness. You set the pace. Honesty breeds honesty. Vulnerability breeds vulnerability. Are you being vulnerable and honest about your own problems and struggles? (This doesn't mean that you have to spill your guts each week or reveal every secret of your life.) Remember, men want an honest, on-their-level leader who strives to walk with God. (Also, as the leader, you need an accountability partner, perhaps another group leader.)

What will we do at the first session?

We encourage you to open by discussing the **Small-Group Covenant** we've included in this resource section. Ask the men to commit to the study, and then discuss how long it will take your group to complete each session. (We suggest 75-90 minute sessions.) Men find it harder to come up with excuses for missing a group session if they have made a covenant to the other men right at the start.

Begin to identify ways certain men can play a more active role in small group. Give away responsibility. You won't feel as burdened, and your men will grow from the experience. Keep in mind that this process can take a few weeks. Challenge men to fulfill one of the group roles identified later in this resource section. If no one steps forward to fill a role, say to one of the men, "George, I've noticed that you are comfortable praying in a group. Would you lead us each week during that time?"

How can we keep the group connected after we finish a study?
Begin talking about starting another Bible study before you finish this eight-week study. (There are six studies to choose from in the Every Man Bible study series.) Consider having a social time at the conclusion of the study, and encourage the men to invite a friend. This will help create momentum and encourage growth as you launch into another study with your group. There are probably many men in your church or neighborhood who aren't in small groups but would like to be. Be the kind of group that includes others.

As your group grows, consider choosing an apprentice leader who can take half the group into another room for the **Connect with the Group** time. That subgroup can stay together for prayer, or you can reconvene as a large group during that time. You could also meet for discussion as a large group, and then break into subgroups for **Standing Strong** and **prayer.**

If your group doubles in size, it might be a perfect opportunity to release your apprentice leader with half the group to start another group. Allow men to pray about this and make a decision as a group. Typically, the relational complexities that come into play when a small group births a new group work themselves out. Allow guys to choose which group they'd like to be a part of. If guys are slow in choosing one group or another, ask them individually to select one of the groups. Take the lead in making this happen.

Look for opportunities for your group to serve in the church or community. Consider a local outreach project or a short-term missions trip. There are literally hundreds of practical ways you can serve the Lord in outreach. Check with your church leaders to learn the needs in your congregation or community. Create some interest by sending out scouts who will return with a report for the group. Serving keeps men from becoming self-focused and ingrown. When you serve as a group, you will grow as a group.

using this study in a large-group format

Many church leaders are looking for biblically based curriculum that can be used in a large-group setting, such as a Sunday-school class, or for small groups within an existing larger men's group. Each of the Every Man Bible studies can be adapted for this purpose. In addition, this curriculum can become a catalyst for churches wishing to launch men's small groups or to build a men's ministry in their church.

Getting Started

Begin by getting the word out to men in your church, inviting them to join you for a men's study based on one of the topics in the Every Man Bible study series. You can place a notice in your church bulletin, have the pastor announce it from the pulpit, or pursue some other means of attracting interest.

Orientation Week

Arrange your room with round tables and chairs. Put approximately six chairs at each table.

Start your class in prayer and introduce your topic with a short but motivational message from any of the scriptures used in the Bible study. Hand out the curriculum and challenge the men to do their homework before each class. During this first session give the men some discussion questions based upon an overview of the material and have them talk things through just within their small group around the table.

Just before you wrap things up, have each group select a table host or leader. You can do this by having everyone point at once to the person at their table they feel would best facilitate discussion for future meetings.

Ask those newly elected table leaders to stay after for a few minutes, and offer them an opportunity to be further trained as small-group leaders as they lead discussions throughout the course of the study.

Subsequent Weeks

Begin in prayer. Then give a short message (15-25 minutes) based upon the scripture used for that lesson. Pull out the most motivating topics or points and strive to make the discussion relevant to the life of an everyday man and his world. Then leave time for each table to work through the discussion questions listed in the curriculum. Be sure the discussion facilitators at each table close in prayer.

At the end of the eight sessions, you might want to challenge each "table group" to become a small group, inviting them to meet regularly with their new small-group leader and continue building the relationships they've begun.

prayer request record

Date:
Name:
Prayer Request:
Praise:

Date:
Name:
Prayer Request:
Praise:

Date:
Name:
Prayer Request:
Praise:

Date:
Name:
Prayer Request:
Praise:

Date:
Name:
Prayer Request:
Praise:

defining group roles

Group Leader: Leads the lesson and facilitates group discussion.

Apprentice Leader: Assists the leader as needed, which may include leading the lesson.

Refreshment Coordinator: Maintains a list of who will provide refreshments. Calls group members on the list to remind them to bring what they signed up for.

Prayer Warrior: Serves as the contact person for prayer between sessions. Establishes a list of those willing to pray for needs that arise. Maintains the prayer-chain list and activates the chain as needed by calling the first person on the list.

Social Chairman: Plans any desired social events during group sessions or at another scheduled time. Gathers members for planning committees as needed.

small-group roster

Name:
Address:
Phone: E-mail:

Name:
Address:
Phone: E-mail:

Name:
Address:
Phone: E-mail:

Name:
Address:
Phone: E-mail:

Name:
Address:
Phone: E-mail:

Name:
Address:
Phone: E-mail:

spiritual checkup

Your answers to the statements below will help you determine which areas you need to work on in order to grow spiritually. Mark the appropriate letter to the left of each statement. Then make a plan to take one step toward further growth in each area. Don't forget to pray for the Lord's wisdom before you begin. Be honest. Don't be overly critical or rationalize your weaknesses.

Y = Yes
S = Somewhat or Sometimes
N = No

My Spiritual Connection with Other Believers

___I am developing relationships with Christian friends.
___I have joined a small group.
___I am dealing with conflict in a biblical manner.
___I have become more loving and forgiving than I was a year ago.
___I am a loving and devoted husband and father.

My Spiritual Growth

___I have committed to daily Bible reading and prayer.
___I am journaling on a regular basis, recording my spiritual growth.

____I am growing spiritually by studying the Bible with others.

____I am honoring God in my finances and personal giving.

____I am filled with joy and gratitude for my life, even during trials.

____I respond to challenges with peace and faith instead of anxiety and anger.

____I avoid addictive behaviors (excessive drinking, overeating, watching too much TV, etc.).

Serving Christ and Others

____I am in the process of discovering my spiritual gifts and talents.

____I am involved in ministry in my church.

____I have taken on a role or responsibility in my small group.

____I am committed to helping someone else grow in his spiritual walk.

Sharing Christ with Others

____I care about and am praying for those around me who are unbelievers.

____I share my experience of coming to know Christ with others.

____I invite others to join me in this group or for weekend worship services.

____I am seeing others come to Christ and am praying for this to happen.

____I do what I can to show kindness to people who don't know Christ.

Surrendering My Life for Growth

___I attend church services weekly.

___I pray for others to know Christ, and I seek to fulfill the Great Commission.

___I regularly worship God through prayer, praise, and music, both at church and at home.

___I care for my body through exercise, nutrition, and rest.

___I am concerned about using my energy to serve God's purposes instead of my own.

My Identity in the Lord

___I see myself as a beloved son of God, one whom God loves regardless of my sin.

___I can come to God in all of my humanity and know that He accepts me completely. When I fail, I willingly run to God for forgiveness.

___I experience Jesus as an encouraging Friend and Lord each moment of the day.

___I have an abiding sense that God is on my side. I am aware of His gracious presence with me throughout the day.

___During moments of beauty, grace, and human connection, I lift up praise and thanks to God.

___I believe that using my talents to their fullest pleases the Lord.

___I experience God's love for me in powerful ways.

small-group covenant

As a committed group member, I agree to the following:*

- **Regular Attendance.** I will attend group sessions on time and let everyone know in advance if I can't make it.
- **Group Safety.** I will help create a safe, encouraging environment where men can share their thoughts and feelings without fear of embarrassment or rejection. I will not judge another guy or attempt to fix his problems.
- **Confidentiality.** I will always keep to myself everything that is shared in the group.
- **Acceptance.** I will respect different opinions or beliefs and let Scripture be the teacher.
- **Accountability.** I will make myself accountable to the other group members for the personal goals I share.
- **Friendliness.** I will look for those around me who might join the group and explore their faith with other men.
- **Ownership.** I will prayerfully consider taking on a specific role within the group as the opportunity arises.
- **Spiritual Growth.** I will commit to establishing a daily quiet time with God, which includes doing the homework for this study. I will share with the group the progress I make and the struggles I experience as I seek to grow spiritually.

Signed: _____ Date: _____

---

* *Permission is given to photocopy and distribute this form to each man in your group. Review this covenant quarterly or as needed.*

about the authors

STEPHEN ARTERBURN is coauthor of the bestselling Every Man series. He is also founder and chairman of New Life Clinics, host of the daily *New Life Live!* national radio program, and creator of the Women of Faith conferences. A nationally known speaker and licensed minister, Stephen has authored more than forty books. He lives with his family in Laguna Beach, California.

KENNY LUCK is president and founder of Every Man Ministries and coauthor of *Every Man, God's Man* and its companion workbook. He is division leader for men's small groups and teaches a men's interactive Bible study at Saddleback Church in Lake Forest, California. He and his wife, Chrissy, have three children and reside in Rancho Santa Margarita, California.

TODD WENDORFF is a graduate of U.C. Berkeley and holds a Th.M. from Talbot School of Theology. He serves as a pastor of men's ministries at Saddleback Church and is an adjunct professor at Biola University. He is an author of the Doing Life Together Bible study series. Todd and his wife, Denise, live with their three children in Trabuco Canyon, California.

CARL MOELLER is the pastor to the singles' communities at Saddleback Church. Carl is a graduate of Trinity Evangelical Divinity School and has a Ph.D. from the University of Utah. Carl and his wonderful wife, Kimberly, have four children and live in Trabuco Canyon, California.

every man's battle workshops

from New Life Ministries

new Life Ministries receives hundreds of calls every month from Christian men who are struggling to stay pure in the midst of daily challenges to their sexual integrity and from pastors who are looking for guidance in how to keep fragile marriages from falling apart all around them.

As part of our commitment to equip individuals to win these battles, New Life Ministries has developed biblically based workshops directly geared to answer these needs. These workshops are held several times per year around the country.

- Our workshops for men are structured to equip men with the tools necessary to maintain sexual integrity and enjoy healthy, productive relationships.

- Our workshops for church leaders are targeted to help pastors and men's ministry leaders develop programs to help families being attacked by this destructive addiction.

Some comments from previous workshop attendees:

"An awesome, life-changing experience. Awesome teaching, teacher, content and program." —Dave

"God has truly worked a great work in me since the EMB workshop. I am fully confident that with God's help, I will be restored in my ministry position. Thank you for your concern. I realize that this is a battle, but I now have the weapons of warfare as mentioned in Ephesians 6:10, and I am using them to gain victory!" —Ken

"It's great to have a workshop you can confidently recommend to anyone without hesitation, knowing that it is truly life changing. Your labors are not in vain!" —Dr. Brad Stenberg, Pasadena, CA

If sexual temptation is threatening your marriage or your church, please call **1-800-NEW-LIFE** to speak with one of our specialists.

every man conferences
revolutionizing local churches

"This is a revolutionary conference that has the potential to change the world. Thanks Kenny! The fire is kindled!" —B.J.

"The conference was tremendous and exactly what I needed personally. The church I pastor is starting a men's group to study the material launched at this conference. This is truly an answer to my prayer!" —DAVID

"Thank you! Thank you! Thank you! I didn't know how much I needed this. I look forward to working through the material with my small group." —BOB

"It's the only conference I have attended where I will go back and read my notes!" —ROGER

"This is a conference every man should attend." —KARL

"After years of waffling with God, I am ready to welcome Him into my every day life. Thanks for giving me the tools to help me develop a relationship with God." —GEORGE

"This revolutionary conference is the next wave of men's ministry in America." —STEVE ARTERBURN, Coauthor of *Every Man's Battle*

If you want to :
- address the highest felt need issues among men
- launch or grow your men's ministry
- connect your men in small groups around God's Word
- and reach seeking men with the Gospel

Join with other churches or sponsor an every man conference in your area.

For information on booking Kenny Luck or scheduling an Every Man Conference contact Every Man Ministries at 949-766-7830 or email at everymanministries@aol.com. For more information on Every Man events, visit our website at everymanministries.com.

start a bible study
and connect with others
who want to be God's man.

If you enjoyed the *Every Man, God's Man Workbook,* you'll love the Every Man Bible Studies, designed to help you discover, own, and build on convictions grounded in God's word.